Dinosaurs

by Wiley Blevins • illustrated by Janet Samuel

Some dinosaurs are big.

Some dinosaurs are little.

Some dinosaurs have spikes.

Some dinosaurs have horns.

Some dinosaurs can fly.

Some dinosaurs can run.

Some dinosaurs are scary!